A Zen Quote A Day

A Zen Quote A Day

365 Existential Zen Quotes For A Zensational Year

Rahul Karn

Rahul Karn

Copyright © 2021 by Rahul Karn

All rights reserved. No part of this book may be reproduced in any manner whatsoever without written permission except in the case of brief quotations embodied in critical articles and reviews.

First Printing, 2021

A
ZEN
QUOTE
A
DAY
A COLLECTION OF 365 ZEN QUOTES

Rahul Karn

Dedicated To
The Buddha

PREFACE

Dear Zen Friends,

There is an ancient saying that an apple a day keeps the doctor away. It ticked me with an idea about trying the same with Zen Stories.

Thanks for welcoming my book 'A Zen Story A Day'. I decided to try the same with the sayings of Zen Masters and here is the book: 'A Zen Quote A Day'.

This book is collection of 365 quotes, one quote for each day of your year. They are compiled from various sources and have been welcomed on my Facebook page 'Zensational Stories' widely in these many years. Facebook brings you the posts you like in pasts years as a memory. Yet I felt a deep need of a book which contains the most important sayings of Zen Masters.

This book contains sayings of various Zen Masters and great philosophers. However, one remarkable thing about some of the philosophers is that they were not Zen Masters. Yet their teachings are most welcome in Zen monasteries. And thus, they have been included in the book, as you will se.

In my first book 'Zensational Stories' I have published many commentaries on classic Zen Stories and Quotes. Many times, people ask me to write commentaries on more stories and quotes. However, I personally feel that the sound of raindrops doesn't need a commentary. In this volume, I am presenting the quotes as they are in the raw form. May be in future books, I might quench the thirst of some of my dear readers. For now, please be happy with the commentary-less version!

One more thing, while it's good to have an apple a day, it's not good for your health to eat all 365 apples in a single day. Similarly, these quotes are also there to be enjoyed slowly. Do not take it as a novel and finish it in one go. It will defeat the purpose of these quotes.

I am sure these stories will be the starting point to take you on a more serious journey of Zen.

Should you have any queries, please don't hesitate to contact me on zensationalstories@gmail.com.

Have a Zensational time ahead!

Your Zen Friend,
Rahul Karn
Canberra
20th of June 2021

1

The Deceptive Buddha

"The Buddhas and ancestors are like deceptive thieves. If you gain some understanding, but are unable to penetrate beyond them, then they have deceived you."

~ Zen Master Xinfeng ~

2

Persistence

"If you have not yet completely awakened, you must go to the meditation cushion and sit impassively for ten, twenty, thirty years, observing your original face before your father and mother were born."

~ Zen Master Taixu ~

3

Becoming Special

"No matter how many years you sit doing zazen, you will never become anything special."

~ Zen Master Sawaki ~

4

Weak and Strong

"Nothing weaker than water. Nothing stronger than rock. Still, a slow flow of water can cut through mountains."

~ Taoist Proverb ~

Beginning of Wisdom

"To know what we do not know is the beginning of wisdom."

~ Maha Sthavira Sangharakshita ~

6

Bare Talking

"It is better to practice a little than to talk a lot."

~ Muso Kokushi ~

7

Experience

"Give back what you have learned. Share your experience."

~ Deng Ming-Dao ~

8

Dance

"Life isn't about waiting for the storm to pass, it's about learning how to dance in the rain."

~ Zen Proverb ~

Better than Silence

"Do not speak- unless it improves on silence."

~ Zen Proverb ~

10

Work Hard on Zazen

"You should pay attention to the fact that even the Buddha Shakyamuni had to practice zazen for six years. It is also said that Bodhidharma had to do zazen at Shaolin temple for nine years in order to transmit the Buddha-mind. Since these ancient sages were so diligent, how can present-day trainees do without the practice of zazen? You should stop pursuing words and letters and learn to withdraw and reflect on yourself. When you do so, your body and mind will naturally fall away, and your original Buddha-nature will appear."

~ Zen Master Dogen ~

11

Seeking

"When one first seeks the truth, one separates oneself from it."

~ Zen Master Dogen ~

12

Reminder

"Man needs more to be
reminded
than instructed."

~ Samuel Johnson ~

13

Option

"If a man has nothing to eat, fasting is the most intelligent thing he can do."

~ Herman Hesse ~

14

Fragrance

"A bit of fragrance always clings to the hand that gives roses."

~ Zen Proverb ~

15

Stupid?

"The people of the world are merry making and contented,
As if enjoying the sacrificial feast.
I alone am mild, like one unemployed.
Like a new-born babe that cannot smile.
All men have enough and to spare;
I alone seem to have lost everything.
Others are sharp and clever;
But I alone am dull and stupid!."

~ Lao Tzu (Tao Te Ching) ~

"Whole world is contented; they eat and sleep. Only Kabir is the discontented one, who remains awake and cries.

Whole world is intelligent, only I became insane!!!"

~ Kabir ~

16

Hurry?

"Nature does not hurry, yet everything is accomplished."

~ Zen Proverb ~

Seeking Delusion

"A great deal of intelligence can be invested in ignorance when the need for illusion is deep!"

~ Saul Bellow ~

Envy

"One shouldn't disparage the gifts one obtains,
Nor crave the possessions that others have gained.
He who envies others does not obtain peace of mind."

~ Buddha (Dhamma Pada, 25/6) ~

19

Wake Up!

"Zen is simply a voice crying, 'Wake up! Wake up!'"

~ Maha Sthavira Sangharakshita ~

20

Quiet

"The quieter you become, the more you can hear."

~ Zen Proverb ~

21

Look

"Who we are looking for, is who is looking."

~ Francis of Assisi ~

22

Tao

"As you start to walk out on the way, the way appears."

~ Rumi ~

23

Simple

"To ask the hard question is simple."

~ W.H. Auden ~

24

Useless

"When we are unable to find tranquillity within ourselves, it is useless to seek it elsewhere."

~ Francois de La Rochefoucauld ~

A Burden

"Remembering a wrong is like carrying a burden on the mind."

~ Buddha ~

26

Boredom

"Boredom: the desire for desires."

~ Leo Tolstoy ~

27

A Painting

"A painting of rice cake does not satisfy hunger."

~ Zen Proverb ~

28

Muddy Water

"Muddy water, let stand, becomes clear."

~ Lao Tzu (Tao Te Ching) ~

29

Learning

"You can't stop the waves, but you can learn how to surf."

~ Jon Kabat-Zinn ~

Two Roads

"Two roads diverged in a wood, and I —
I took the one less travelled by,
And that has made all the difference."

~ Robert Frost ~

No Confusion

"Zen does not confuse spirituality with thinking about God while peeling potatoes. Zen is just peeling potatoes."

~ Alan Watts ~

32

A Green Tree

"Keep a green tree in your heart and perhaps a singing bird will come."

~ Zen Proverb ~

The Ignorant Man

"The ignorant man is an ox. He grows in size, not in wisdom."

~ Buddha ~

34

The Reality

> "As long as you seek for something,
> you will get the shadow of reality,
> and not reality itself."
>
> ~ Shunryu Suzuki ~

35

Something

"I'd like to offer something to help you but in the Zen school we don't have a single thing!"

~ Ikkyu ~

36

Nothingness

"The true art of enlightenment is seeing into nothingness. When I look in my wallet, I am enlightened."

~ Roshi So ~

37

Knock! Knock!!

"Knock on the sky and listen to the sound."

~ Zen Proverb ~

38

Searching

"When you seek it, you cannot find it."

~ Zen Proverb ~

39

Enough

"There is no greater affliction than desire, no greater curse than discontent, no greater misfortune than wanting something for oneself. Therefore, he who knows that enough is enough will always have enough."

~ Lao Tzu (Tao Te Ching) ~

40

Everyone

"On whose door does the moonlight not shine!"

~ Zen Proverb ~

The Way

"What good are doctrines? The ultimate Truth is beyond words. Doctrines are words. They're not the Way. The Way is wordless.
Words are illusions."

~ Bodhidharma ~

42

Silence

"Let silence take you to the core of life."

~ Rumi ~

43

And You?

"And you? When will you begin that long journey into yourself?"

~ Rumi ~

Dissatisfaction

"The root of dissatisfaction:
always looking for the next thing."

~ Dzogchen ~

Suffering

"'He insulted me, he harmed me,
he robbed me, he beat me.'
If you think like this, you will suffer.
'He insulted me, he harmed me,
he robbed me, he beat me.'
If you don't think like this, you won't suffer."

~ Buddha ~

Beyond Words

"Where can I find a man
who has forgotten words?
He is the one I would like to talk to."

~ Chuang Tzu ~

Pointing the Way

"The masters only point the way.
But if you meditate
and
follow the dharma
you will free yourself."

~ Buddha ~

Nothing Done

"When nothing is done,
nothing is left undone."

~ Zen Proverb ~

Becoming

"Do not attempt to become the Buddha."

~ Zen Master Dogen ~

50

Easy

"The bird of paradise lands only on the hand that does not grasp."

~ Zen Proverb ~

Zen is Poetry

"Zen is not a philosophy, it is poetry.
It does not propose, it simply persuades.
It does not argue, it simply sings its own song."

~ Osho ~

Here it is

"Clouds gone; the mountain appears."

~ Zen Proverb ~

53

Spectacles

"Zen is like looking for the spectacles that are sitting on your nose."

~ Zen Proverb ~

54

Knowledge is Action

"To know and not to do is not to know."

~ Zen Proverb ~

55

The Infinite

"The infinite is in the finite of every instant."

~ Zen Proverb ~

Present Enough?

"Guilt, regret, resentment, sadness & all forms of non-forgiveness are caused by too much past & not enough presence."

~ Eckhart Tolle ~

Buddha in Marketplace

"Dig deep into your own being -- be enriched by it! And bring that flavour back to the periphery. Bring that fragrance back to the world. Bring that aura, that light, that grace, that dignity, that grandeur, back to the periphery.
Walk in the marketplace like a Buddha."

~ Osho ~

You are Here

"You may have a million desires to be in other places, doing other things, but you are not there, you are here."

~ Zen Proverb ~

59

Mind It

"No enemy, no hater can harm you
as much as your own ill-directed mind can.
Not a mother, nor a father, nor any other
relative can do more for your well-being than
your own rightly-directed mind can."

~ Buddha (Dhammapada) ~

No Nonsense

"Unless you see your nature, all this talk about cause & effect is nonsense.
Buddhas don't practice nonsense."

~ Bodhidharma ~

form
Possession

> "What you possess, you lose."
>
> ~ Zen Proverb ~

Fear of Unknown

"People have a hard time letting go of their suffering. They prefer suffering that is familiar to the unknown."

~ Thich Nhat Hanh ~

63

Grow Up

"All people on the planet are children, except for a very few. No one is grown up except those free of desire."

~ Rumi ~

Awareness

"There are men who walk through the woods and see no trees."

~ Mongolian Proverb ~

65

Self

"Just keep coming home to yourself. You are the one you've been waiting for."

~ Byron Katie ~

Who

"Who would you be without your story?"

~ Byron Katie ~

/ 67

Come

"I know you're tired but come, this is the way."

~ Rumi ~

Investment

"The greatest stock market you can invest in is yourself. Finding this truth is better than finding a gold mine."

~ Byron Katie ~

Ego

"The problem is that ego can convert anything to its own use, even spirituality."

~ Chogyam Trungpa ~

Happiness

"Happiness is the natural state for someone who knows that there's nothing to know."

~ Byron Katie ~

71

Too Clear

"Since it is all too clear, it takes time to grasp it."

~ Zen Proverb ~

Ordinary

"One teacher said, 'ordinary mind is the way.' Another said, 'no mind is the way.' I ended up having 'no ordinary mind.'"

~ Roshi So ~

73

Gone

"No matter how much you try to hold on to something, it will all be gone."

~ Taoist Proverb ~

74

Hope & Fear

"Hope and fear cannot alter the seasons."

~ Chogyam Trungpa ~

The Truth

"The truth is: you don't have a life, you are life."

~ Eckhart Tolle ~

76

Knowledge

"The less a man knows, the surer he is that he knows everything."

~ Joyce Cary ~

Beware

"If you would not turn your back on the Way,
do not follow the world."

~ Takuan ~

78

Ready

"When the student is ready, the master appears."

~ Zen Proverb ~

79

Meeting

"Wherever I go, I meet myself."

~ Shunryu Suzuki Roshi ~

80

Forget

"Forget all your concepts. All that you have learned about truth is false."

~ Huang Po ~

81

Calm

"It is easy to have calmness in inactivity, it is hard to have calmness in activity, but calmness in activity is true calmness."

~ Shunryu Suzuki ~

82

Return

"All words and sayings gently turn, returning to the self."

~ Bassui ~

83

The Familiar

"The familiar,
precisely because it is familiar,
remains unknown."

~ Hegel ~

84

Desires

"If you obtain what you desire, does it make you happy?"

~ Scott Shaw ~

85

Don't Be A Camel

"If you become a camel,
they'll put a load on your back."

~ Mongolian Proverb ~

Understanding

"If you use your mind to study reality,
you won't understand
either your mind or reality.
If you study reality without using your mind,
you'll understand both."

~ Bodhidharma ~

87

Happy

"If you want to be happy, be."

~ Aleksey Tolstoy ~

88

Theory

"Theoretical knowledge has no end."

~ Chokyi Nyima Rinpoche ~

Just Meditate

"If you have a glass full of liquid you can discourse forever on its qualities, discuss whether it is cold, warm, whether it is really and truly composed of H-2-O, or even mineral water, or saki. Meditation is drinking it!"

~ Taisen Deshimaru ~

Rationale

"Every uncomfortable feeling, every pain, every moment of stress & suffering is for your own self-realization."

~ Byron Katie ~

Concentration

"Concentration is not
staring hard at something.
It is not trying to concentrate."

~ W. Timothy Gallwey ~

Start Walking

"All know the Way,
but few actually walk it."

~ Bodhidharma ~

93

Tourists

"We are all here on this planet as tourists.
None of us can live here forever."

~ Dalai Lama ~

Pain

"Where there is anger,
there is always pain underneath."

~ Eckhart Tolle ~

Gold

"Although gold dust is precious,
when it gets in your eyes,
it obstructs your vision."

~ Hsi-Tang ~

Practice Awareness

"Normally, we do not so much look at things as overlook them."

~ Alan Watts ~

Let It Go

"The next time you have a thought... let it go."

~ Ron White ~

The Fundamental Delusion

"The fundamental delusion of humanity
is to suppose that I am here,
and you are out there."

~ Yasutani Roshi ~

But

"It is true,
the wind blows terribly here -
but moonlight
also leaks between the roof planks
of this ruined house."

~ Izumi Shikibu (974-1034) ~

100

The Key

"Success is not the key to happiness.
Happiness is the key to success."

~ Albert Schweitzer ~

101

Peace

"Peace in ourselves,
peace in the world."

~ Thich Nhat Hanh ~

The Reward

"The journey is the reward."

~ Taoist Proverb ~

Punishment

"You will not be punished for your anger;
you will be punished by your anger."

~ Buddha ~

104

Kinhin

"Every path, every street in the world is your walking meditation path."

~ Thich Nhat Hanh ~

Good Will

"With good will for the entire cosmos,
cultivate a limitless heart & mind:
Beaming above, below, & all around,
unobstructed, without trace of hostility."

~ Buddha (Metta Sutta) ~

Befriending

"Meditation practice isn't about trying to throw ourselves away and become something better. It's about befriending who we are already."

~ Pema Chödrön ~

107

Not Understanding

"Although you may
understand the explanations,
if you are still suffering because of problems,
you clearly do not understand the true nature
of your mind, your body, and your senses."

~ Lama Zopa Rinpoche ~

108

Peaceful

"A crust eaten in peace is better than a banquet partaken in anxiety."

~ Aesop ~

Zazen

"I have discovered that all of man's unhappiness derives from only one source,
not being able to sit quietly in a room."

~ Blaise Pascal ~

//110

Real Charity

"You perform real charity if you can give freely without expecting anything in return."

~ Buddha ~

Pain

"Pain is inevitable as long as you are identified with your mind."

~ Eckhart Tolle ~

112

Fooled

"When you are fooled by something else,
the damage will not be so big.
But when you are fooled by yourself, it is fatal.
No more medicine."

~ Shunryu Suzuki ~

Summary

"Understand
the suffering of worldly existence.
Abandon
its causes of ignorance and selfishness.
Practice
the path of meditation and compassion.
Awaken
from suffering within Great Peace."

~ Buddha ~

The Real Cause

"If I think that someone else
is causing my problem,
I'm insane."

~ Byron Katie ~

115

Look

> "Don't think:
> Look!"
>
> ~ Ludwig Wittgenstein ~

A Unique Lover

"When you become a lover of what is,
the war is over."

~ Byron Katie ~

117

A Tragedy

"It is the tragedy of the world
that no one knows what he doesn't know."

~ Joyce Cary ~

Interest

"Be at least as interested in what goes on inside you as what happens outside."

~ Eckhart Tolle ~

The Perfect Teacher

"This very moment is the perfect teacher, and lucky for us,
it's with us wherever we go."

~ Pema Chodron ~

120

Nothing

"Nothing outside you can ever give you what you're looking for."

~ Byron Katie ~

Victim

"When you believe that your problem
is caused by someone or something else,
you become your own victim."

~ Byron Katie ~

Doing Nothing

"Take the time to just do nothing.
It will open up a completely new world
of insight for you."

~ Scott Shaw ~

Practice

"Do not entertain hopes for realization
but practice all your life."

~ Milarepa ~

Awakening

"Who looks outside,
dreams.
Who looks inside,
awakes."

~ Carl Gustav Jung ~

Let It Settle

"No thought, no reflection,
no analysis, no cultivation,
no intention;
let it settle itself."

~ Tilopa ~

126

Witnessing

"Be the witness of your thoughts."

~ Buddha ~

127

Stillness

"Stillness and tranquillity set things in order in the universe."

~ Lao Tzu ~

Fountain

"There is a fountain inside you.
Don't walk around with an empty bucket."

~ Rumi ~

Don't Delay

"The affairs of the world will go on forever.
Do not delay the practice of meditation."

~ Milarepa ~

A Unique Monastery

"In the monastery of your heart and body,
you have a temple where all buddhas unite."

~ Milarepa ~

A Unique Study

"I study my mind and therefore all appearances are my texts."

~ Milarepa ~

Counting

"Not everything that can be counted counts,
and not everything that counts can be counted."

~ William Bruce Cameron ~

Meditate Regularly

"The more regularly and the more deeply you meditate, the sooner you will find yourself acting always from a centre of inner peace.

~ J. Donald Walter ~

Clarity

"When the pools of perception are clear, everything appears 'as is'."

~ Zen Proverb ~

135

The Purpose of Meditation

"Meditation is not meant to help us avoid problems or run away from difficulties. It is meant to allow positive healing to take place. To meditate is to learn how to stop—to stop being carried away by our regrets about the past, our anger or despair in the present, or our worries about the future."

~ Thich Nhat Hanh ~

The Real Freedom

"The wise ones, ever meditative
and steadfastly persevering,
alone experience Nibbana,
the in-comparable freedom from bondage."

~ Buddha (Dhammapada) ~

Zen Tea

"Drink your tea slowly and reverently, as if it is the axis on which the earth revolves – slowly, evenly, without rushing toward the future. Live the actual moment. Only this moment is life."

~ Thich Nhat Hanh ~

Mindfulness

"One who takes delight in mindfulness
and sees danger in heedlessness,
advances like fire, burning up all fetters, great
and small."

~ Buddha (Dhammapada) ~

Meditation Brings Wisdom

"Meditation brings wisdom; lack of meditation leaves ignorance. Know well what leads you forward and what holds you back."

~ Buddha ~

Music

> "When I am silent
> I fall into that place
> where everything is music."
>
> ~ Rumi ~

Know the Thinker

"When you no longer believe everything you think, you step out of thought and see clearly that the thinker is not who you are."

~ Eckhart Tolle ~

Observe your Thoughts

"Don't wish to become a future Buddha;
Your only concern should be,
As thought follows thought,
To avoid clinging to any of them."

~ Dogen ~

An Observation

"After meditating for some years,
I began to see the patterns
of my own behaviour.
As you quiet your mind, you begin to see
the nature of your own resistance more clearly,
struggles, inner dialogues, the way in which
you procrastinate and develop passive resistance against life.
As you cultivate the witness, things change.
You don't have to change them.
Things just change."

~ Ram Dass ~

144

Peace

"Being still does not mean don't move.
It means move in peace."

~ E'yen A. Gardner ~

Intellectualization

"As soon as you see something,
you already start to intellectualize it.
As soon as you intellectualize something,
it is no longer what you saw."

~ Shunryu Suzuki ~

Meditative Awareness

"Meditation, simply defined,
is a way of being aware.
It is the happy marriage of doing and being."

~ Lama Surya Das ~

147

Emotion

"An emotion is only an emotion. It's just a small part of your whole being. You are much more than your emotion. An emotion comes, stays for a while, and goes away, just like a storm. If you're aware of that, you won't be afraid of your emotions."

~ Thich Nhat Hanh ~

The Present Moment

"To dwell in the here and now does not mean you never think about the past, or responsibly plan for the future. The idea is simply not to allow yourself to get lost in regrets about the past or worries about the future. If you are firmly grounded in the present moment, the past can be an object of inquiry, the object of your mindfulness and concentration. You can attain many insights by looking into the past, but you are still grounded in the present moment."

~ Thich Nhat Hanh ~

149

Your Own Nature

"To find a Buddha all you have to do is see your nature."

~ Bodhidharma ~

No Excuses

"Five minutes Zazen,
five minutes Buddha.
One minute Zazen,
one minute Buddha.
Just sit: no excuses."

~ Zen Saying ~

151

Zen

"Zen can be described as:
A special transmission outside the scriptures,
Not based upon words or letters;
Directly pointing to the mind
Seeing into one's true nature, attaining the Buddha way."

~ Anonymous ~

152

The Ultimate Bravery

"The ultimate definition of bravery is not being afraid of who you are."

~ Chogyam Trungpa ~

The Silent Teaching

"The Dhamma is revealing itself in every moment, but only when the mind is quiet can we understand what it is saying, for the Dhamma teaches without words."

~ Ajahn Chah ~

Breathing

"Practicing meditation is just like breathing. While working we breathe, while sleeping we breathe, while sitting down we breathe... Why do we have time to breathe? Because we see the importance of the breath, we can always find time to breathe. In the same way, if we see the importance of meditation practice, we will find the time to practice."

~ Ajahn Chah ~

155

Words

"If whatsoever you have been living can be conveyed by words, that means you have not lived at all."

~ Osho ~

156

Peaceful

"If we are peaceful, if we are happy,
we can smile and blossom like a flower,
and everyone in our family,
our entire society, will benefit from our peace."

~ Thich Nhat Hanh ~

157

Know Thyself

"You know everything about the world,
but you do not know anything about yourself.
This is a ridiculous way to live!"

~ Sadhguru ~

Start Meditating

"Start with meditation and things will go on growing in you - silence, serenity, blissfulness, sensitivity. And whatever comes out of meditation, try to bring it out in life. Share it, because everything shared grows fast."

~ Osho ~

The Real Enemy

"If you want to get rid of your enemy, the true way is to realize that your enemy is delusion."

~ Buddha ~

Something Missing

"You're just suffering from the belief that there's something missing from your life."

~ Byron Katie ~

The Great Teacher

"The highest truth cannot be put into words.
Therefore, the greatest teacher has nothing to say;
He simply gives himself in service, and never worries."

~ Hua Hu Ching, Verse 23 ~

Witnessing

"Meditation starts by being separate from the mind, by being a witness. That is the only way of separating yourself from anything. If you are looking at the light, naturally one thing is certain: you are not the light, you are the one who is looking at it. If you are watching the flowers, one thing is certain: you are not the flower, you are the watcher.

Watching is the key of meditation.

Watch your mind.

Don't do anything - no repetition of mantra, no repetition of the name of God - just watch whatever the mind is doing. Don't disturb it, don't prevent it, don't repress it; don't do anything at all on your part. You just be a watcher, and the miracle of watching is meditation. As you watch, slowly mind becomes empty of thoughts;

but you are not falling asleep, you are becoming more alert, more aware."

~ Osho ~

A Zen Saying

"In Japan the Zen people have a saying:
'It is mind that deludes mind
for there is no other mind.
Oh mind, do not let yourself
be misled by mind.'
Kokoro koso,
kokoro mayowasi,
kokoro nare;
kokoro ni,
kokoro,
kokoro yurusu na."

~ Osho: Zen, The Path of Paradox Vol. 1 ~

Confusion

"I've come to see that confusion is the only suffering on this planet."

~ Byron Katie ~

Entertainment

"Man needs entertainment simply to hide his madness. If he was perfectly sane, he would not need entertainment. He could just sit and watch this bamboo grow. He does not really need entertainment."

~ Sadhguru ~

Rest

"Find that place which is effortlessly at rest within itself. Be there—be one with that."

~ Mooji ~

Silence Please

"Not till your thoughts cease all
their branching here and there,
Not till you abandon all thoughts
of seeking for something,
Not till your mind is motionless
as wood or stone, will you be
on the right road to the Gate."

~ Huang Po ~

Teacher

"Wherever you go you will find your teacher, as long as you have the eyes to see and the ears to hear."

~ Shunryu Suzuki ~

Awesome Stillness

"Meditation is to be still: to sit still, to stand still, and to walk with stillness.
Meditation means to look deeply, to touch deeply so we can realize we are already home.
Our home is available right here and now.
When we learn to stop and be truly alive in the present moment,
we are in touch with what's going on within and around us."

~ Thich Nhat Hanh ~

Witness

"Just know what is happening in your mind – not happy or sad about it, not attached. If you suffer see it, know it, and be empty."

~ Ajahn Chah ~

171

A Teaching

"Meditation will not carry you to another world, but it will reveal the most profound and awesome dimensions of the world in which you already live. Calmly contemplating these dimensions and bringing them into the service of compassion and kindness is the right way to make rapid gains in meditation as well as in life."

~ Anonymous ~

Mind Matters

"Says Zen:
In Spring hundreds of flowers
In Autumn a harvest moon
In Summer a refreshing breeze
In Winter snow will accompany you.
If useless things do not hang in your mind
Any season is a good season to you."

~ Osho: Zen, The Path of Paradox, Vol 1 ~

Life

"Life is available only in the present. That is why we should walk in such a way that every step can bring us to the here and the now."

~ Thich Nhat Hanh ~

174

Intimacy

"Enlightenment is intimacy with all things."

~ Zen Master Dogen ~

Sometimes

"Sometimes your joy is the source of your smile,
but sometimes your smile can be the source of your joy."

~ Thich Nhat Hanh ~

No Prayers, No Scriptures

"I have not heard of a single Buddha, past or present,
who has been enlightened by sacred prayers and scriptures."

~ Bassui ~

Hell

"When the mind is always moving, you travel from one hell to the next hell."

~ Bodhidharma ~

The Real Master

"Worldly fools search for exotic masters
not realizing that
their own mind is the master."

~ Bodhidharma ~

Attachment

"It's not the appearance that binds you, it's the attachment to the appearance that binds you."

~ Tilopa ~

Disappointment

"What people expect to happen
is often different from what actually happens.
Thus, does disappointment arise.
This is the way the world works."

~ Buddha ~

Futile Seeking

"Why do you so earnestly seek
the truth in distant places?
Look for delusion and truth in the
bottom of your own heart."

~ Ryokan ~

Shape Yourself

"Irrigators guide water;
fletchers straighten arrows;
carpenters bend wood;
wise people shape themselves."

~ Buddha ~

183

Incomparable

"No light is comparable to the light of wisdom."

~ Buddha ~

184

Yelling

"If you're yelling within you that they shouldn't yell at you, that is where the pain begins, not with their yelling at you."

~ Byron Katie ~

The Liar Buddha

"Tell a lie
And you will fall into hell.
Then what will happen to Buddha
Who contrived
Things that don't exist?"

~ Zen Master Ikkyu ~

True Religion

"My religion is not deceiving myself."

~ Milarepa ~

Heaven

"You were searching for a heaven, mm? That's what people have been doing down the ages. They don't change themselves, they hanker for a heaven, but wherever they go they will create hell. They ARE hell -- it is not a question of finding heaven somewhere.
Unless you have it already in you, you will not find it anywhere.".....
"Unless you are a bodhisattva,
wherever you are you will be in hell.
When passion is transformed
into compassion....
Then, wherever you are, you are in heaven.
That is the only paradise there is."

~ Osho: The Diamond Sutra ~

Thought

"How much of life do you let pass by without a thought?"

~ Scott Shaw ~

Looking Outside

"We've been looking outside us for our own peace.
We've been looking in the wrong direction."

~ Byron Katie ~

Reflection

"The whole moon and the entire sky are reflected in one dewdrop on the grass."

~ Zen Master Dogen ~

Existence

"I exist nowhere
in the universe.
But in the universe,
there is nothing which is not me."

~ Zen Saying ~

Benediction

"With stillness comes the benediction of peace."

~ Eckhart Tolle ~

Remain with The Moment

"Mind always goes ahead or lags behind. Remain with the moment."

~ Osho : Meditation, The First And Last Freedom ~

Zen is Experiential

"Zen is experiential. It is not a talk about great things, it is not a philosophy. It is a very simple and obvious phenomenon – just to look in. What can be more simple?

As you look in, a totally new world opens its doors and your old language becomes irrelevant. All that you can say is, the old is finished.

The new is discontinuous with the old. Neither the language nor any gesture, nothing can manage the new in the form that the old allows.

The new brings its own language.

The new brings its own home.

The new brings your ultimate reality."

~ Osho: Joshu, The Lion's Roar ~

Footsteps

"Do not seek to follow in the footsteps of the men of old; seek what they sought."

~ Basho ~

Dead Scriptures

"Any scripture to which nothing can be added is dead."

~ Osho ~

Zazen on The Mountain

"The birds have vanished from the sky.
Now the last cloud rains away.
We sit together, the mountain and me,
until only the mountain remains.

~ Li Po (701-762) ~

Innocence

"Until you see the world as innocent, you haven't realized your own innocence."

~ Byron Katie ~

Experience Yourself

"Once you have tasted flight, you will forever walk the earth with your eyes turned skyward, for there you have been, and there you will always long to return."

~ Leonardo da Vinci ~

Be Sure

"Be sure that what you want is right for you to have."

~ Buddhist Proverb ~

Problems

"Man unnecessarily creates problems. I want you to understand that there are no problems in life except those you create. Because your ego needs problems."

~ Osho ~

Ignorance

"Where ignorance is our master, there is no possibility of real peace."

~ Dalai Lama ~

# Settlement

"If you know that fundamentally there is nothing to seek, you have settled your affairs."

~ Rinzai ~

The Watcher on The Hill

"Rather than being
your thoughts and emotions,
be the awareness behind them."

~ Eckhart Tolle ~

Thoughts

"Be empty of worrying. Think of who created thought!"

~ Rumi ~

206

Weird Zen

"Zen takes food from a hungry man and the sword from a soldier."

~ Nyogen ~

Images

"A thousand lakes have a thousand images of the moon. If there is no cloud in the sky, the heaven extends itself boundlessly."

~ Zen Saying ~

Story

"It's only when I believe a story that I get hurt. And I'm the one who's hurting me by believing what I think."

~ Byron Katie ~

Just Relax

"Don't seek, don't search, don't ask, don't knock, don't demand – relax."

~ Osho: Zen The Path Of Paradox, Vol 1 ~

210

Perfect

"A hundred flowers follow the first bloom;
They will festoon each field and garden.
The eastern breeze blows gently everywhere;
Each branch has the perfect color of spring."

~ Genro ~

Why Worry?

"Worry is like a rocking chair, it will give you something to do, but it won't get you anywhere."

~ Anonymous ~

Ego

"Ego is constantly attempting to acquire and apply the teachings of spirituality for its own benefit."

~ Chogyam Trungpa ~

The Seashore Mind

"Footsteps in the sand, quickly washed away:
The seashore mind."

~ Deng Ming-Dao ~

214

Limitless

"The sky isn't the limit; the mind that sees the sky is the limit."

~ Byron Katie ~

215

No Scriptures

"If one relies on words in various Buddhist texts,
the meaning of the Buddha cannot be attained!"

~ Hui-Neng, The Sixth Zen Patriarch ~

216

Disappear

"A heavy snowfall disappears into the sea.
What silence!"

~ Zen Saying ~

217

Understand the Mind

"Until we understand the mind, we suffer!"

~ Byron Katie ~

218

The Quest

"The truth is not a question. It is a quest! It is not intellectual; it is existential. The inquiry is a gamble, a gamble with your life. It needs tremendous courage. Belief needs no courage.
Belief is the way of the coward. If you are a Christian or a Hindu or a Mohammedan you are a coward."

~ Osho: The First Principle ~

Equanimity

"He whose mind does not flutter by contact with worldly conditions (Gain and loss, honour and disgrace, praise and blame, happiness and pain), Sorrowless, Stainless, and Secure - this is the Highest Blessing."

~ Buddha ~

220

Don't Betray

"Don't betray the ancient sages' compassion."

~ Zen Master Wuzu Fayan (1024-1104) ~

Mind

> "The hustle and bustle
> of the mind in karma:
> Within it is
> Nirvana."

~ Zenrin Kushû ~

222

The Hidden Treasure

"To waste all day
in the busy town,
Forgetting the treasure
in his own house."

~ Zenrin Kushû ~

223

Awesome Clarity

"Those who want to understand the source of life and death must first clearly understand their own selves. Once they're clear about this, then afterward they can act appropriately according to circumstances, never missing the mark."

~ Zen Master Huitang Zuxin (1025-1100) ~

224

It Happens

"Sitting quietly doing nothing, the spring comes and grass grows by itself."

~ Zen Saying ~

The Hardest Thing

"The hardest thing to see is what is in front of your eyes."

~ Johann Wolfgang von Goethe ~

226

Laughter

"The nightmare always becomes laughter, once it's understood."

~ Byron Katie ~

Protect Yourself

"If one holds oneself as dear,
one protects oneself.
During any of the three watches (of life viz.
childhood, youth and old age) the wise man
would stay awake (guarding himself)."

~ Buddha ~

228

Don't Be Stupid

"You can repeat the most profound words ever uttered, and you can still be a stupid man."

~ Osho: And The Flowers Showered ~

Preaching Zen

"Rain bamboos,
wind pines:
all preach Zen."

~ A Zen Forest: Zen Sayings ~

Love

"With life as short as a half-taken breath,
don't plant anything but love."

~ Rumi ~

231

Peace and Joy

"If you can find peace and joy staring at a wall you can find it anywhere."

~ Chad Foreman ~

232

Utilize Your Time

"Sitting in a public bus or in a railway train, when you have nothing to do, just close your eyes. It will save your eyes from being tired from looking outside, and it will give you time enough to watch yourself."

~ Osho: Awareness, The Key to Living in Balance ~

Plop!

> "The old pond
> A frog jumps in.
> Plop!"

~ Haiku by Basho ~

Rebellion

"We have to fight around the world against all kinds of priests and all kinds of politicians. It is a question of the very survival of freedom on the earth."

~ Osho: Zen: The Diamond Thunderbolt ~

235

Be Selfish

"Just enjoy it
yourself:
It's not for giving
to anyone else."

~ Zenrin Kushû ~

Look Within

"One cannot grasp the meaning by turning to words, paper and ink."

~ Zen Saying ~

Stink

"Hard to realize it's
the stink of his own shit!"

~ Zenrin Kushû ~

Be Responsible

"Do not follow the ideas of others
but learn to listen to the voice within yourself.
Your body and mind will become clear
and you will realize the unity of all things."

~ Zen Master Dogen ~

Ghost

"Let the world call you lazy for not running about like a frightened ghost. Just be quiet inside yourself. Don't bother about knowing how things should be and simply begin observing without prejudice, projections or desires. Notice how life flows of its own accord. Nothing here is a chaos, but a harmony. You are already inside this flow."

~ Mooji ~

The Devil

"Look for Buddha outside your own mind, and Buddha becomes the devil."

~ Zen Master Dogen ~

Just Meditate

"Prayer is always addressed to somebody else.
Prayer is not religious.
Worship is not religious.
Being fully aware and silent is the only way of knowing the taste of religion."

~ Osho: Zen, The Quantum Leap From Mind To No Mind ~

Enjoy

"Every meditation is a preparation for enjoying the aloneness which is our nature."

~ Osho: The Language Of Existence ~

The Way

"If you want to travel the Way
of Buddhas and Zen masters,
then expect nothing,
seek nothing,
and grasp nothing."

~ Zen Master Dogen ~

No Gain

"I gained nothing at all from Supreme Enlightenment, and for that very reason it is called Supreme Enlightenment."

~ Buddha ~

Exploitation

"All the religions have exploited your hidden desires."

~ Osho: The Messiah, Vol 1 ~

246

Zen Soap

"Zen is like soap. First you wash with it, and then you wash off the soap."

~ Yamaoka Tesshu ~

Stress

"Stress is an ignorant state. It believes that everything is an emergency. Nothing is that important."

~ Natalie Goldberg ~

248

Patience

"Do you have the patience to wait
till the mud settles and the water is clear?
Can you remain without reaction
till the right action arises by itself?"

~ Lao Tzu (Tao Te Ching) ~

Wonderful Sight

"Where sun and moon
cannot reach -
There
is a wonderful sight."

~ A Zen Forest: Zen Sayings ~

It Is What It Is!

"Mountains are mountains;
water, water."

~ Zenrin Kushû ~

Nature

"The old pine
talks Zen;
The calm bird
whispers satori."

~ Zenrin Kushû ~

Opinions

"Do not seek the truth, only cease to cherish your opinions."

~ Seng-ts'an ~

253

Celebration

"You never bother about who is hidden inside you, what is the source of your being.
Those who have known the source, they are unanimously in agreement that it is the most precious experience that can happen in this world. It is the most universal which gives you a deathlessness, and which gives your life a tremendous freshness, and in each moment a radiance, a grace, a beauty. Your whole life becomes a celebration."

~ Osho: Turning In ~

The Teachers We Need

"My experience is that the teachers we need most are the people we're living with right now."

~ Byron Katie ~

Views

"People suffer because they are caught in their views. As soon as we release those views, we are free and we don't suffer anymore."

~ Thich Nhat Hanh ~

Die

"Die each moment to the past and be born again. Each breath that goes out should be your death, and each breath that comes in should be your life. If you can live with so much change, like a river flowing, you are always fresh, you are always original; your clarity is absolute, you are transparent."

~ Osho: Live Zen ~

The Buddha Demon

"If you seek the Buddha, you will be caught by the Buddha Demon; if you seek the patriarchs, you will be bound by the patriarch-Demon.
Whatever you are seeking,
all becomes suffering."

~ Zen Master Rinzai ~

Meditate

"Enlightenment cannot be found in books or sutras or in performing rituals. Rather, it is to be found within the self through meditation."

~ Bodhidharma ~

Impermanence

"A man says a lot of things in summer he doesn't mean in winter."

~ Patricia Briggs ~

Presence

"Meditation is offering your genuine presence to yourself in every moment."

~ Thich Nhat Hanh ~

Enlightenment

"Enlightenment can be multidimensional. It can include laughter, it can include love, it can include beauty, it can include creativity. There is nothing to keep it from the world and from transforming the world into a more poetic place, a more beautiful garden. Everything can be brought to a better state of grace."

~ Osho: Rinzai, Master of The Irrational ~

Beautiful Innocence

"Meditation gets you into a space where mind is left behind with all its knowledge. Suddenly you start functioning from a state of not-knowing, from innocence. And that innocence is beautiful and that innocence is fragrant. That innocence is the essential religion."

~ Osho: Walking in Zen, Sitting in Zen ~

Inflation

"It may seem, in times of inflation, that all prices are going up, but the price of living remains the same - death."

~ Zen Without Zen Master by Camden Benares ~

Naturally

"When the wind blows, the grasses bend."

~ John Daido Loori's notes on Dogen's 300 Koans ~

Detachment

"Until I loved my thoughts, I couldn't love the world."

~ Byron Katie ~

Guideless

"Coming, going, the waterfowl
Leaves not a trace.
Nor does it need a guide."

~ Zen Master Dogen ~

Fun

"Some children have caught a mouse and now it's writhing in the trap. They're having fun watching how it scrapes its nose till it bleeds and how it rips up its tail . . . In the end they'll throw it to the cat for food. If I was sitting in the mouse's place, I'd say to myself, 'You damn humans won't have any fun with me!' And I'd simply sit Zazen."

~ Kodo Sawaki Roshi ~

Egotists

"The more I study religions the more I am convinced that man never worshiped anything but himself."

~ Richard Francis Burton ~

Be Present

"Nothing ever happened in the past that can prevent you from being present now."

~ Eckhart Tolle ~

Disidentify from Your Mind

"The single most vital step on your journey toward enlightenment is this: learn to disidentify from your mind. Every time you create a gap in the stream of mind, the light of your consciousness grows stronger.

One day you may catch yourself smiling at the voice in your head, as you would smile at the antics of a child. This means that you no longer take the content of your mind all that seriously, as your sense of self does not depend on it."

~ Eckhart Tolle ~

Laziness

"Most people, in fact, will not take the trouble in finding out the truth, but are much more inclined to accept the first story they hear."

~ Thucydides (460 - 400 BC) ~

Forest

"The forest is peaceful, why aren't you? You hold on to things causing your confusion. Let nature teach you. Hear the bird's song then let go. If you know nature, you'll know Dhamma. If you know Dhamma, you'll know nature."

~ Ajahn Chah ~

The Destination

"Before a step is taken,
you have already arrived.
Before a word is spoken,
the truth has been expressed."

~ John Daido Loori ~

Acceptance

"You suffer because you don't want to accept what has to be accepted."

~ Kodo Sawaki Roshi ~

Translation

"The sound of the rain needs no translation."

~ Zen Saying ~

Stillness of Mind

"When mind is still, then truth gets her chance to be heard in the purity of the silence."

~ Sri Aurobindo ~

Moment to Moment

"The future is completely open, and we are writing it moment to moment."

~ Pema Chodron ~

All-Pervasive Silence

"If you walk into a forest - you hear all kinds of subtle sounds - but underneath there is an all-pervasive silence."

~ Eckhart Tolle ~

Let It Happen

"Let what comes come.
Let what goes go.
Find out what remains."

~ Ramana Maharshi ~

Urgent

"In the age of constant movement, nothing is so urgent as sitting still."

~ Pico Iyer ~

Go Slowly

"Smile, breathe and go slowly."

~ Thich Nhat Hanh ~

Eyes

"The real voyage of discovery consists not in seeking new landscapes, but in having new eyes.

~ Marcel Proust ~

Depth

"Though the wave of words is forever upon us,
yet our depth is forever silent."

~ Kahlil Gibran ~

Quietude

"There is always music amongst the trees in the garden, but our hearts must be very quiet to hear it."

~ Minnie Aumonier ~

Greatest Service

"Your own self-realization is the greatest service you can give the world."

~ Ramana Maharshi ~

286

Totality

"Wherever you are, be there totally."

~ Eckhart Tolle ~

Renunciation

"Renunciation is not getting rid of the things of this world,
but accepting that they pass away."

~ Robert Aitken ~

Apple and Zen

"Zen is not interested in high-flown statements;
it wants its pupil to bite his apple and not discuss it."

~ Ann Bancroft ~

Worship

"You can worship Gods,
but you cannot worship Tao."

~ Ming-Dao Deng ~

290

Be Diligent

"Ah, be diligent! Be diligent! Of a thousand or ten thousand attempting to enter by this Gate, only three or perhaps five pass through. If you are heedless of my warnings, calamity is sure to follow. Therefore, is it written:
Exert your strength in THIS life to attain!
Or else incur long aeons of further pain!

~ Huang-Po, The Wan Ling Record ~

291

Trust in Change

"Yesterday's wisdom is today's foolishness.
Trust only in change."

~ Ikkyu ~

Observe

"To meditate does not mean to fight with a problem. To meditate means to observe."

~ Thich Nhat Hanh ~

Crazy Wisdom

"It's logical;
if you're not going anywhere
any road is the right one."

~ Ikkyu ~

Surrender

"The plants and flowers
I raised about my hut
I now surrender
To the will
Of the wind."

~ Ryokan ~

Happiness

"Happiness is the absence of the striving for happiness."

~ Zhuangzi ~

Liberate Yourself

"Beings liberate themselves by knowing their own mind. Buddhas don't liberate anyone. If Buddhas could liberate beings, since you've already met countless Buddhas, why haven't you become a Buddha?"

~ Huiko ~

The Meaning

"One falling leaf is not just one leaf; it means the whole autum."

~ Zen Saying ~

298

Learn Your Lesson

"Nothing ever goes away until it has taught us what we need to know."

~ Pema Chodron ~

… 299

Dreams

"Since I Am Convinced
That Reality Is In No Way
Real,
How Am I To Admit
That Dreams Are Dreams?"

~ Saigyo Hoshi ~

Deep Inside

"At the surface, the mind plays so many games - thinking, imagining, dreaming, giving suggestions. But deep inside the mind remains a prisoner of its own habit patterns."

~ World Vipassana Teacher S. N. Goenka ~

Essence

"People have the illusion of being conscious when in reality they are asleep, essentially unconscious, with no true self or identity which they can call their own."

~ Gurdjieff ~

The World

"Most people in China will not care much if a monk does not follow the
precepts, has little or no virtue, drinks alcohol, or eats meat.
But if a monk is seen to interact with a woman, then everyone will make a big
deal out of it."

~ Venerable Hsing Yun ~

The True Power of Zen

"Those who study the Path must become again like infants. Then praise and blame, success and fame, unfavourable circumstances, unfavourable environments -- none of these can move them. Though their eyes see form, they're the same as a blind person. Though their ears hear sound, they're the same as a deaf person. They're like fools, like idiots. The mind is motionless as Mount Sumeru. This is the place where patch-robed monastics and practitioners really attain true power."

~ Master Yuanwu ~

Pleasure and Pain

"Pleasure is not a reward. Pain is not a punishment. They're just ordinary occurrences."

~ Chogyam Trungpa Rinpoche ~

305

Ignorance

"Not knowing that I must leave everything and depart,
I did various ill deeds for the sake of friend and foe."

~ Buddha ~

What is it?

"What is this mind?
Who is hearing these sounds?
Do not mistake any state for
Self-realization, but continue
To ask yourself even more intensely,
What is it that hears?"

~ Bassui ~

Investigation

"Pain shows you what's left to investigate."

~ Byron Katie ~

308

Enjoy the Journey

"Focus on the journey, not the destination. Joy is found not in finishing an activity but in doing it."

~ Greg Anderson ~

Now

"I am not my thoughts, emotions, sense perceptions, & experiences. I am not the content of my life. I am life. I am the space in which all things happen. I am consciousness. I am the now."

~ Eckhart Tolle ~

First Experience It

"To accept some idea of truth without experiencing it
is like a painting of a cake on paper which you
cannot eat."

~ Shunryu Suzuki ~

Humble

"People who've had any genuine spiritual experience always know that they don't know. They are utterly humbled before mystery. They are in awe before the abyss of it all, in wonder at eternity and depth, and a Love, which is incomprehensible to the mind."

~ Richard Rohr ~

Love

"Life is nothing but an opportunity for love to blossom."

~ Osho: The Rebellious Spirit ~

No Intoxicants

"There are those who say, 'An occasional drink won't hurt anyone.' But an occasional drinker is still a drinker. It is rather like the state of being 'a little pregnant.' Either there is a pregnancy or there isn't. The description "occasional" is an unlocked door which any thief can enter. Either sobriety's door is locked, or it isn't... The occasional drinker can remain sober when he is not beset by problems; but as soon as he's under serious stress, he may easily succumb to the dead-end escape of alcohol. Once he is captured by drink, he discovers that one drink is too many and a hundred drinks are not enough."

~ Zen Master Xu Yun ~

Mystery

"As we acquire more knowledge, things do not become more comprehensible, but more mysterious."

~ Will Durant ~

# Sorry

"According to ancient wisdom, 'The thief is sorry he is to be hanged - not that he is a thief.'"

~ Zen Master Xu Yun ~

The Secret of Meditation

"Think the unthinkable. How to think the unthinkable? Be without thoughts-this is the secret of meditation."

~ Zen Master Dogen ~

Losing

"You can only lose something that you have,
but you cannot lose something that you are."

~ Eckhart Tolle ~

The Real Miracle

"People say walking on water is a miracle, but to me walking peacefully on earth is the real miracle."

~ Thich Nhat Hanh ~

Bless Thyself

"You are the source of your own happiness. Only your blessings can ease the pain in your heart."

~ Gary Zukav ~

320

Zen

"Zen isn't a matter of fashion!"

~ Zen Master Ikkyu ~

321

Zen is Alive

"The doctrine consists of dead words, while Seon (Zen) is alive."

~ Korean Zen Master Baekpa Geungseon (1767-1852) ~

322

Zen is Not Thinking

"Thinking about awakening produces only thoughts."

~ Zen Proverb ~

Paradox of Life

"No one who has fallen to the earth
has ever arisen without depending on the
earth."

~ Zen Saying ~

Attainment

"Originally there is
nothing to be attained."

~ Bodhidharma ~

325

Zazen

"If the students rely on written texts and language as their Way, this is like a lamp in the wind: not being able to dispel darkness, the flames wither and die. [But if you] sit still with nothing the matter; it is like a lamp in a hidden room that dispels the darkness and clearly distinguishes things."

~ Dazu Huike, The Second Patriarch Of Zen ~

Harmony with Nature

"Don't live by your own rules, but in harmony with Nature."

~ Epictetus ~

The True Pilgrimage

"To stop simply hanging on to what has been in the past and longing for what might be in the future is better than making a ten-year pilgrimage."

~ Zen Master Rinzai ~

Ordinary

"Just be ordinary, wearing your clothes and eating your food, passing your time without concerns. All of you coming from various directions, you all have minds fixed on something. You seek the Buddha, or you seek the Truth; you seek liberation and transcendence of the mundane world. Fools! If you want to leave this ordinary world, where are you going to go?"

~ Zen Master Rinzai ~

Koan

"Meditate continuously twenty-four hours a day and do not let there be any interruptions. Arise long before dawn, gather up the koan, and put it before you. If you feel the least bit sleepy, get up from the meditation seat and walk around, still with your attention on the koan. With every step you take while walking, do not depart from the koan. Whether spreading out your mat, or holding out your bowl, or lifting up your spoon, or putting down your chopsticks, or following along with the congregation, never depart from the koan. Carry on like this all through the day and all through the night. All those who fuse themselves into one whole with the koan will surely develop illumination."

~ Zen Master Gaofeng Yuanmiao ~

Spontaneous Illumination

"The experience described as shedding your skin, transcending reflections of subjective awareness, where no mental machinations can reach, is not transmitted by sages. It can only be attained inwardly, by profound experience of spontaneous illumination. The original light destroys the darkness, real illumination mirrors the infinite. Subjective assessments of what is or is not are all transcended."

~ Zen Master Hongzhi ~

Truth

"Do not think that the knowledge you presently possess is changeless, absolute truth. Avoid being narrow-minded and bound to present views. Learn and practice non-attachment from your views in order to be open to receive other's viewpoints. Truth is found in life and not merely in conceptual knowledge. Be ready to learn throughout your entire life and to observe reality in yourself and in the world at all times."

~ Thich Nhat Hanh ~

Excitement?

"Zen is not some kind of excitement, but concentration on our
usual everyday routine."

~ Shunryu Suzuki ~

333

Zazen on The Mountain

"All the birds have flown up and gone;
A lonely cloud floats leisurely by.
We never tire of looking at each other
Only the mountain and I."

~ Li Po ~

Tea Break

"Meditation was a labour, all night long,
But when you brewed tea, I felt infinitely glad.
Just one cup of tea, and the dark clouds were banished,
Feeling cool to my very bones, all worry vanished."

~ Korean Zen Master Muuija (1178-1234) ~

Revelation

"Mountains and rivers
and the great earth:
Everything reveals
the Body of Buddha."

~ Zenrin Kushû ~

336

Abusing The Buddha

"If one regards the witnessed Dharma as having names and characteristics that
can be preached, this is not an understanding of the holy intention, and is called ABUSING the Buddha."

~ The Jin'gang xianlun (Clear Treatise on the Diamond Sutra) ~

No Doctrine

"When Buddhas and Zen masters appear in the world, everything they say, all their various techniques, expounding Zen and the teachings, are without exception tools for breaking attachments according to the situation; basically, there is no real doctrine to give people."

~ Han-shan ~

Mind is Buddha

"The wise know that mind is Buddha, while the ignorant wish for paradise."

~ Pao-chih ~

The Murderer Buddha

"A buddha has to be both -- a murderer and a mother. On the one hand he has to kill, on the other hand he has to give new being to you. The new being is possible only when the old has been destroyed. Only on the ashes of the old the new is born... Man is the being who has to die to be reborn."

~ Osho: The Diamond Sutra ~

340

Live Zen

"In general students should investigate the live sentences and should not
investigate the dead sentences.
If you understand the live sentence, then you can be a teacher for the
Buddha and patriarchs; if you understand the dead sentence, you will be
unable to save yourself."

~ The Great Master Seosan Hyujeong (1520-1604) ~

Attachment

"In order to remove the attachment to beings,
The Tathāgata taught emptiness.
If one, in turn, becomes attached to emptiness,
[Even] the Buddhas cannot transform such a person."

~ Wonhyo(617-686) ~

Waiting

"Let me define meditation: meditation is waiting
without prospect, waiting for waiting's sake.

~ Osho: The Sun Rises in The Evening ~

Set Aside

"Set aside all the slogans you have learned and all the intellectual views that stick to your skin and cling to your flesh. Make your mind empty, not manifesting any thoughts on your own, not doing anything at all."

~ Yuanwu ~

Egotism

"Many worldly intellectuals just study Zen for something to talk about, something that will enhance their reputation. They consider this a lofty interest and try to use it to assert superiority over others. This just increases egotism."

~ Yuanwu ~

Great Doubt

"Mengshan (Deyi) said, 'In the investigation of Chan, it is a major fault not to doubt words and sentences.' He also said, 'With great doubt you are certain to have great enlightenment.'"

~ The Great Master Seosan Hyujeong
(1520-1604) ~

Slippery Tongue

"Even if you immediately have a great insight and a great awakening, and can talk like clouds and rain, all you have gained is a slippery tongue—you are further and further from the way. That's what is called being a whore for appearances."

~ Ch'eng-ku ~

Continuity

"My teacher said, 'When you are asleep, study Zen as you sleep. When you are eating, study Zen as you eat.'"

~ Foyan ~

Idea

"Zen is not a conception—if you set up an idea of it, you turn away from the source."

~ Shoitsu ~

Conceptual Study

"To study Zen conceptually is like drilling in ice for fire, like digging a hole to look for the sky. It just increases mental fatigue. To study Zen by training is adding mud to dirt, scattering sand in the eyes, impeding you more and more."

~ Yuanwu ~

350

Worshipping Won't Help

"If you think you can become enlightened just by worshiping images and relics, this is a mistaken view. This is actually possession by the poisonous serpent of temptation."

~ Zen Master Dogen ~

Enlightened

"Years of digging the earth searching for the blue sky,
piling up layer upon layer of mediocrity.
Then one dark night the ceiling blew off,
and the whole structure disappeared into emptiness."

~ Muso Soseki ~

The Most Important Thing

"The most important thing is to find out what is the most important thing."

~ Shunryu Suzuki ~

Incense

"To Buddha:
the more incense the better?"

~ Zenrin Kushû ~

Sickness

"If you hope to keep a still mind,
You haven't yet avoided sickness."

~ Niu-t'ou Fa-yung (594-657) ~

Revelation

"The Buddha is the Essence of your being; outside it there is no Buddha."

~ Hui Neng, The Sixth Patriarch of Zen ~

356

Just Meditate

"If one could attain complete liberation from life and death
By merely chanting the names of Buddha,
What is the use of diligently practicing the Sixteen Meditation Samadhi?
Such practice is against the teachings of Buddha and will never succeed."

~ The Great Seon Master Gyeongheo
(1846-1912) ~

Strange Zen

"Zen monks are strange fellows. If one says white, then the other says black. They have no intention of contradicting one another. Their purpose is to show a colourless colour."

~ Nyogen ~

Bright Light

"Ch'an (Zen), if applied in our daily lives, would be like a ship in
the sea of suffering. It would be like a bright light in the darkness."

~ Ch'an Master Hsing Yung ~

359

Work Hard on Meditation

"Dropping off body and mind is good practice. Make a vigorous effort to pierce your nostrils."

~ Zen Master Dogen ~

Not Done

"If one does not actually realize the truth of Zen in one's own experience, but simply learns it verbally and collects words, and claims to understand Zen, how can one solve the riddle of life and death?"

~ Huang Po ~

Experience Yourself

"The teachings, the philosophies, the explanations of the Buddhist path really don't have any worth at all. The worth is all contained in the experiencing."

~ Phakchok Rinpoche ~

Zen Remains

"Masters come and go, disciples come and disappear;
Zen remains.
Just as it is.
It is always just as it is."

~ Osho: Live Zen ~

363

Every Step Peaceful

"The mind can go in a thousand directions.
But on this beautiful path, I walk in peace.
With each step, a gentle wind blows.
With each step, a flower blooms."

~ Thich Nhat Hanh ~

Unending Peace

"Throughout the universe
there is unending peace!"

~ Zen Master Dogen ~

365

The End

"When you end your internal war, that is the end of all war."

~ Byron Katie ~

BONUS. The End?

"At the beginning nothing comes,
In the middle nothing stays,
In the end nothing goes."

~ Milarepa ~

Bibliography

1. The Zen Teaching of Bodhidharma, Translated by Red Pine
2. The Record of Rinzai
3. Zen's Chinese Heritage by Andy Ferguson
4. Records of the Transmission of the Lamp (Jingde Chuandeng Lu, Vol 1-8) by Daoyuan, translated by Randolph S. Whitfield
5. Treasury of the Forest of Ancestors by Satyavayu
6. Zen Flesh, Zen Bones by Nyogen Senzaki and Paul Reps
7. Dogen's 300 Koans
8. Shobogenzo by Dogen
9. Zen Speaks: Shouts of Nothingness by Tsai Chih Chung

10. The Original Teachings of Ch'an Buddhism by Chang Ching Yuan
11. The Golden Age of Zen: Zen Masters of the T'ang by John Ching Hsiung Wu
12. Zen, The Path of Paradox, Vol 1-3 by Osho
13. A Bird on the Wing by Osho
14. (Collected Works of Korean Buddhism, Volume 3) Hyujeong, Selected Works Edited and Translated by John Jorgensen
15. (Collected Works of Korean Buddhism, Volume 7-1) Gongan Collections I Edited and Translated by John Jorgensen
16. (Collected Works of Korean Buddhism, Volume 7-2) Gongan Collections II Edited and Translated by John Jorgensen
17. (Collected Works of Korean Buddhism, Volume 8) Seon Dialogues, Edited and Translated by John Jorgensen
18. Being Peace by Thich Nhat Hahn
19. Records of Yunmen (Master Yunmen, From the Record of the Chan Teacher "Gate of the Clouds" published by Kodansha International)
20. The Warrior Koans

21. The Buddha, The Emptiness Of The Heart by Osho
22. Zen: The Mystery and The Poetry of The Beyond by Osho
23. A Sudden Clash of Thunder by Osho
24. Meditating with Koans by Zhuhong, Translated by J. C. Cleary
25. The Zen Reader by Thomas Cleary
26. Kyozan, A True Man of Zen by Osho
27. Zen: The Quantum Leap from Mind to No Mind by Osho
28. Japanese Death Poems by Yoel Hoffman
29. The Iron Flute: 100 Zen Koans by Nyogen Senzaki, Ruth Strout-McCandless
30. The Zen Doctrine of No-Mind by D. T. Suzuki
31. Zen and Zen Classics, Vol 3, by R.H. Blyth
32. Every End Exposed: The 100 Koans of Master Kido - With the Answers of Hakuin – Zen
33. The Zen Teaching of Huang Po on the Transmission of Mind, Translated by John Blofeld

34. Zen Mind, Beginner's Mind by Shunryu Suzuki
35. Google

www.ingramcontent.com/pod-product-compliance
Lightning Source LLC
Chambersburg PA
CBHW071952290426
44109CB00018B/2000